MILLIONAIRE

 MILLIONAIRE

# MILLIONAIRE

MILLIONAIRE

 MILLIONAIRE

# INDEX

**Introduction**

**Why Claims Are Important to Finance**

**How to Use Affirmations Effectively for the Millionaire**

**How to Get Started**

**Affirmation of the millionaire mentality**

**Affirmation of Income Fixation**

**Affirmation of the attraction**

**Cash Magnet Affirmation**

**Affirmation of Easy Money**

**Conclusion**

 MILLIONAIRE

 MILLIONAIRE

# Introduction

Rich individuals think differently than the middle class and the poor class, in all aspects of life, but above all, when it comes to money. The rich think and act in a determined way, which leads them to have an attitude of wealth, beliefs and positions that produce fortune.

With these new attitudes come new options and consecutively this will produce a cataract of opportunities for them, where all the time they will obtain wealth, thanks to their multiple sources of income.

 MILLIONAIRE

# Why Claims Are Important to Finance

**Empowerment**

Affirmations are statements where an individual speaks to himself and is, begin to produce powerful effects in the subconscious.

These visualizations are viewed as "credible" and are placed in the subconscious area which has to do with the power to enhance the ability to employ particular powerful memories with less work.

 MILLIONAIRE

Through these special images a person can develop the internal tools to think about money differently, letting the memories and images be transported to the here and now, where they are used to improve the way you see the money that is crucial to finances and their empowerment.

Why do we need affirmations for financial empowerment? Often individuals believe that these good and beneficial memories of self communication are a false belief and do not exist, but the subconscious recognizes where they are located and will direct them forward to increase success in finance and life.

These forms of affirmation/suggestions pioneer the fresh neural tracts in the mind, improving the ability to "play" with these

 MILLIONAIRE

fresh and powerful images. Toxic visualizations related to negativity, weaknesses, initiative deficiency, images of fragile targets and the ability to develop and work a financial action plan are reduced. When the mind discovers hearing new claims of self-talk, the subconscious sees it as "tangible".

You have probably noticed a common element in those who are rich, in finances and in life. These winners and successful people tend to be enthusiastic and jealous in all aspects of their lives. This vicious exuberance tends to infect all those with whom the successful individual interacts. A positive attitude, and the power to turn that attitude into results is crucial to seizing new opportunities, acquiring the best of financial decisions and working with goal setting, both in business and in life.

 MILLIONAIRE

As you can see, a positive attitude is a valuable asset, no matter where you are in the financial world. This means that you must assume the habit of exercising regular positive affirmations. Making positive affirmations a part of your daily function is a great way to alter your thoughts and help yourself become more financially successful.

It is never too early or too late to start this cycle of positive affirmations, and even those who have just started a financial plan can benefit from a positive attitude. Even if your position seems insignificant and you are not yet rich, it is crucial to show a positive attitude, and not let negativity sneak in to steal your enthusiasm. Remember that some of the richest people and business owners started from the bottom up. It is really

 MILLIONAIRE

possible to go from a small bank account to being rich, but without positive affirmations and a victorious attitude, this step will not be possible.

Constant positive affirmations are extremely crucial for those who want to achieve financial empowerment. Gaining wealth is never simple, but it is crucial to remember that those around you, from the people you interact with to customers and competitors, feel your attitude and use it as a signal. If you constantly complain about the lack of money and the deficiency of knowing how to be rich, the people around you will be less than invigorated. If, on the other hand, you are constantly providing positive affirmations to yourself and the people around you, even in the most difficult moments, they will see your exuberance, learn from it, and use it as a signal to work harder and help develop your

 MILLIONAIRE

wealth. It really comes down to the proactive attitude it leads to and positive affirmations that can help their financial empowerment.

 MILLIONAIRE

# How to Use Affirmations Effectively for the Millionaire

### Mentality

Affirmations are simple to create and use, but you need dedication to make them work. Here are some suggestions to help you make the most of these powerful tools for new riches.

Affirmations work... But they must be used correctly

Self-affirmations are positive affirmations or

 MILLIONAIRE

scripts of your own that can condition the subconscious so that you can develop a more positive perception of yourself and how you see wealth. Affirmations can help you change adverse behaviors or achieve financial empowerment, and they can also help undo the damage caused by negative scripts, those things that we tell ourselves repeatedly, or that others tell us repeatedly and that add up to negative self-perception and a vision of money in scarcity.

Consider their positive attributes. Take stock of yourself by making a list of your best qualities, abilities or additional properties. Are you thrifty? Do you budget well with your money? If you answer these questions affirmatively using the present tense: "I'm thrifty," for example, or "I'm a good budget," these statements are statements of who you are. We rarely revolve around things we

 MILLIONAIRE

sincerely like about ourselves, but choose to think about things we would like to alter. A list will help you break that cycle, and using these statements to help you appreciate who you are will give you the confidence you need to accept your claims of financial power.

Consider what negative scenarios you would like to neutralize or what positive financial goals you would like to achieve. Affirmations can be very helpful in countering the negative perceptions you have acquired about your ability to manage or attract money. Affirmations can also help you achieve specific financial goals, such as buying a home or a new car. Make a list of your goals or adverse self-perceptions that you would like to alter.

 MILLIONAIRE

Prioritize your list of issues you should work on. You may find that you have many goals or require many different affirmations.

It is best, however, to revolve around a couple of statements at a time, so choose the most crucial or urgent ones and work with them first. When you see improvements in those areas or reach those goals, you can make new statements for other items on your list.

Write down your statements. Use the positive statements only as counter-writings, or add other statements to shape your behavior with and about money in the future. The statements you will use to shape future changes should follow the same form. They should begin with "**I**," and be concise, clear, and positive. There are two forms of forward-

 MILLIONAIRE

looking statements that you can use to work toward goals:

- I can" statements are statements that affirm the fact that you can achieve your goal(s). For example, if you want to contribute $1,000,000 a month, a statement like "I can contribute $1,000,000 a month" is a good start. Several experts recommend that you avoid any form of negative connotation.

- Yes, I will" statements are a statement stating that today you will really use your ability to achieve your goal. So, following the example above, you can say, "I will bring $1,000,000 this month. Again, you must use positive language and clearly state what you will do today to achieve the long-term goal of financial empowerment and wealth.

 MILLIONAIRE

Compare some of your positive attributes with your goals. Which of the positive characters will help you achieve your goals? For example, if you're dealing with ways to stick to a budget, you may need willpower or courage. Select statements to support what you will need.

Make your repetitions visible so you can use them. Repetition is the key to effective statements. You want to consider your statements several times a day and on an ongoing basis, if required.

Proceed using your affirmations. The more you affirm something, the more firmly your mind will accept it. If you are trying to achieve a short-term goal, use your

 MILLIONAIRE

affirmations until you have achieved it. Remember that the universe hears everything, so be careful with your affirmations. Words are oral or written speeches that carry great weight in your life.

Don't use negative words. Instead of "not wanting not to have money," use "I WANT to be rich. The universe does not understand negative thoughts; only "thoughts" are sent to the universe and send the right message. Repetition creates habits and your subconscious mind will align with your desires.

 MILLIONAIRE

# How to Get Started

We can positively change ourselves by changing our thoughts and beliefs. Thoughts are like magnets, they have the power to attract according to their vibration.

What we affirm to ourselves on a daily basis confirms how we feel and experience life. One of the most powerful ways to create the life and wealth we want is through affirmations.

A powerful way to begin using affirmations for financial empowerment is to write them on an index card and read them throughout the day. The more you practice them, the

 MILLIONAIRE

deeper the new beliefs will be. The best times to review your statements are early in the morning, during the day, and before going to bed. After relaxing in a deep, quiet, meditative state of mind, imagine that you have already become rich and know how to manage your money. Imagine the physical environment you would like to be in, the house you would love to have and that comforts you, the mansalva numerical digits it contains in your domain, and the proper financial reward for your work efforts. Add any other details that are essential to you, such as the bills you want to pay, the amount of money you want to earn monthly, and so on. Try to feel in yourself that this is possible; experience it as if it were already happening. In short, imagine it exactly as you would like it to be, as if it were already so. Try to stand in front of a mirror and use affirmations while looking into your eyes. If you can, repeat them out loud with passion. This is a

 MILLIONAIRE

powerful way to change your limiting beliefs very quickly.

If you find it hard to believe that a statement is going to happen, add "I choose" to the statement. "I choose to manage my finances correctly," for example, or "I choose to acquire financial power and become rich.

Tie positive emotions to your statements. Consider how achieving your goal will make you feel, or consider how good it feels to know you're securing your financial future. Emotion is a fuel that makes claims more powerful.

If you don't want people to know about your financial empowerment claims, simply place your reminders in discreet places.

 MILLIONAIRE

Remember, though, that it's essential that you see them often, or they won't do you any good.

If you find yourself simply repeating the words in your affirmations, instead of focusing on their meaning, change the affirmations. You are able to affirm the same objectives or characteristics naturally, but reformulating your affirmations can regenerate their effectiveness.

Ask your friends to tell you a version of their affirmations, for example, "LOLITA, you're really learning how to manage your money. You must feel great." Self-statements are valuable just as they free you from dependence on the approval of others, but the claims of others can be as good as the negative scripts of others are harmful.

 MILLIONAIRE

Gratitude is a very powerful statement, and an example of this can be one that says, "I enjoy the wealth I have in my life, and I trust that more will come my way.

 MILLIONAIRE

# Affirmation of the millionaire mentality

I have a millionaire mentality, money comes to me...

What secrets do the rich know? What kind of mystical powers do they have? The answer is easy. It's all in the way they think. Wealthy individuals have a million-dollar mentality. It is this way of thinking that separates successful souls from the rest of the population.

The subconscious is very powerful. It is much more powerful than your conscious mind. It

 MILLIONAIRE

can help you achieve your dream or prevent you from achieving the success you desire in business and in life.

There are things you can do today that could alter your thinking and give you financial power. Accept absolute responsibility for everything that happens in your life. Stop blaming others for all your problems. Focus on the positive; attract anything you pay attention to. This means that if you focus on what you want, in the end you will get it.

Enjoy your work. Are you trying to be rich by spending fifty or more hours a week doing something you hate? You can only succeed in life if you do what you enjoy. To be genuinely successful, you have to discover your own voice and make your own way.

 MILLIONAIRE

Love yourself. Trust that you have as much right to be happy as others. Trust that you deserve nothing more than the best life has to offer and you will surely be rich.

Never be jealous of the success of others. If you see someone with a fancy car or a beautiful house, say something like "Good for him! Being jealous or envious will only prevent money and wealth from entering your life. Do you want to get rich? Do you want to change your current situation? First of all, you have to create a millionaire mentality by following the instructions above. Soon, miracles will begin to happen in your life and the blessings of wealth and abundance will begin to flow.

MILLIONAIRE

# Affirmation of Income Fixation

## Achieving Income goals

We all have dreams of achieving our ideal income, but without a plan and action they will persist as simple dreams.

This section contains a couple of major steps to achieve your goals and reach the income level you want:

1- Visualize where you would like to be within a year.

 MILLIONAIRE

**2-** Visualize the specific level of business you want and what characteristics it will have. Choose a business that is realistic in terms of the income or profits you want. Visualize as specific as you can.

**3-** Visualize the environment, that is, imagine your ideal clients or team members. Make the visualization of your ideal a daily routine.

**4-** Make a map of the steps you will have to take to be anywhere within a year.

**5-** Think of the obstructions and the ways in which you will overcome them.

**6-** Distinguish your negative thoughts

 MILLIONAIRE

towards the achievement of your business and planned income. When you realize the thoughts that can limit your progress, you will be able to control and defeat them.

**7-** Take steps to reach your goals and expect to get the best out of the things with which you limit your potential.

Come up with a written plan of what it takes to be where you want to be. When you imagine, visualize the ideal, when you plan, do it with truly concrete steps and actions and move forward with them. Get mentors and ask for advice from those who are in the position you want.

Mentors can also be those who are outside your chosen business path and who will help

you be the best. Study the motivational content and keep a positive outlook.

 MILLIONAIRE

# Affirmation of the attraction

I attract new business and opportunities for myself every day

Millions of people have heard of the law of attraction, a theory that provides "positive thinking." Although it is a fairly recent phenomenon, spiritual thinkers say they have been examining concepts for years.

The law of attraction is that our thinking brings us and imparts everything we think. It is as if every time we think a thought, every time we utter a word, the universe is

listening and responding to us.

Neglectivity can prevent you from receiving the things you want in life. Alternatively, you are able to metamorphose your life by remaining positive. You have to start saying things that really feel good about yourself, like: "I enjoy who I am," "I enjoy life," "I like life. You have to understand that you're not going to get it the day of the beginning, but if you plant the seed of good and water it and go ahead with the affirmations, things will begin to transform. Know what you want and ask the universe. This is where you need to be clear about what you would like to create and visualize what you want as true.

Feel and act as if the object of your desire is on its way. Focus your thoughts and your language on what you would like to attract.

MILLIONAIRE

Feel the sensation of truly knowing that what you desire is on its way to you.

Be hospitable in receiving it. Pay attention to your intuitive messages, synchronizations and signs of the Universe to help you along the path as a guarantee that you are on the "right" path. As you consolidate your positive affirmations, the universe will bestow glory upon you.

 MILLIONAIRE

# Cash Magnet Affirmation

**<u>I'm a magnet that attracts money!</u>**

Take a dollar out of your pocket. Notice the green ink and the number on each corner. It's a piece of paper with ink, a couple of numbered symbols, that's all. Individuals work to death to get those green papers. Many live in extreme poverty, all because of the way they see green paper.

Many do not recognize that money is energy. Everything in the cosmos is. We understand that things are different as these energies are vibrating at varying frequencies. Money is not immune to this general law. When the 2

 MILLIONAIRE

energies are harmonic, they attract each other. If not, they repel each other. That is why there are so many poor people. They are not harmonized with money, so they block its flow in their lives. To attract cash you have to be in harmony with it.

We develop thoughts or accept them from an external source, charge them with emotion and inculcate them in the subconscious. We send impulses that are answered by the Universe. Hard work is considered normal. You are subconsciously disciplined to believe that work is the medium through which you get money. The more you work the more money you receive. Individuals were not meant to work twenty hours a day. Nor should they sacrifice themselves to work in three jobs. God did not give us a finite sum of time here on earth to work as slaves. Not with our mental power.

 MILLIONAIRE

I don't want to belittle the idea of work. When we think, we get what we want. By action we receive it. Theoretically we have the ability to manifest money or whatever we want if we are in perfect harmony with the cosmos. Work, but never feel that you have to work or that you need to work for money. This sets up a channel for wealth: your work. The Universe has countless channels. Dedicate time to work, but also dedicate time to thought. Your thought produces your reality.

Money will flow into your life when you allow it. If your cash flow is low, it is stopping the flow. You have negative ideas about money. Possibly you think it is bad. Or that you need to work hard to get it. There are more restrictive beliefs about cash than I

can list here. Negative thoughts block the flow of energy. Positive thoughts let energy flow. When you are aware of any limiting beliefs, you can release them. The key is to discover them.

Cash is a kind of energy, just like you. When these two energies are in harmony, the possibilities are limitless. There are no limits in the Universe, only those that individuals create for themselves.

# Affirmation of Easy Money

**<u>Making money is easy</u>**

We have all been told or heard at some point in our lives that if you sincerely believe in something, have faith in what will happen.

Now there are many individuals who don't believe that idea completely and then there are those who say they practice it, but in reality they don't practice it, they just think they do. Then there are those who sincerely practice the Faith and have tremendous success. Have you ever wondered why or

 MILLIONAIRE

how they do it? There are a number of steps involved in belief and you really need to have everything in place before I can help you reach your goals.

Let me ask you a couple of easy questions:

1- Do you think, without a doubt, that you can and will have everything you want in life?

2- Do you think, without a doubt, that you will be guided to the right situation at the right time?

3- Do you think, without a doubt, that there is always a way to reach your goals?

 MILLIONAIRE

If you answered NO, or perhaps to some of the above questions, that you don't believe and, consequently, you won't get where you want to be; believing requires this complete confidence that everything will work. That you will do your part in finding solutions while you trust and know that you can and will get what you want out of life. So how do we get to that level? You have to get there in small steps. Start setting small goals, even with issues that you know will happen and then trust and resign. You can do this when you are driving, trust that you will get to your destination on time and have a simple round trip. Let's see what happens after a week of doing this. If you lose your keys, tell yourself that you know where they are and trust that you will find them at the right time. If you are unsure of a decision you have to make, consider all the possibilities and then tell yourself that you are making the right decision.

MILLIONAIRE

After a while, by nature, you will consider it again and easily come to a conclusion. The key is to believe and give up. Sometimes you have to be distracted so as not to worry. Worrying is the opposite of believing, that is, I don't believe, so I have to worry - because I can do better by worrying - but you cannot.

I advise you to start small to develop this practice. Like when big decisions have to be made, you'll know the process works and you won't worry, you'll believe you can and will do what you need to do and achieve your goals.

This procedure is so easy and yet so powerful, but it takes time to acquire the habit. This practice of believing is vital to

your financial success. Without it, everything else you do won't make sense in the end.

# Conclusion

Everyone wants to have FINANCIAL POWER. This is a goal that many people have achieved and many more individuals want to achieve. There are many ways to be financially successful, and each individual has his or her own definition of wealth. Regardless of your definition of wealth, affirmations can help you reach your goal.

We hope this Ebook has given you the tools to take a different view of the use of affirmations for financial empowerment.

 MILLIONAIRE

Visit our author page on Amazon and get more **MENTES LIBRES!**

http://amazon.com/author/menteslibres

If you wish, you can leave a comment on this book by clicking on the following link so that we can continue to grow! Thank you very much for your purchase!

https://www.amazon.com/dp/B08264HHH5

www.ingramcontent.com/pod-product-compliance
Lightning Source LLC
Chambersburg PA
CBHW070841220526
45466CB00002B/843